Bats

Written by Adrienne Mason

Illustrated by Nancy Gray Ogle

KIDS CAN PRESS

WILDLIFE SERIES

Kids Can Press

For Ailsa —AM
To my brother, David —NGO

I would like to thank Jenna Dunlop, Ph.D., for her manuscript review and consultation. As always, it was a pleasure to work with the Kids Can team and, in particular, with my editor Stacey Roderick.

Kids Can Press acknowledges the financial support of the Ontario Arts Council, the Canada Council for the Arts and the Government of Canada, through the BPIDP, for our publishing activity.

Published in Canada by
Kids Can Press Ltd.
29 Birch Avenue
Toronto, ON M4V 1E2

Published in the U.S. by
Kids Can Press Ltd.
2250 Military Road
Tonawanda, NY 14150

www.kidscanpress.com

Edited by Stacey Roderick
Designed by Marie Bartholomew
Printed in Hong Kong, China, by Book Art Inc., Toronto

The hardcover edition of this book is smyth sewn casebound.
The paperback edition of this book is limp sewn with a drawn-on cover.

The map appearing on page 9 is courtesy of WorldAtlas.com.

CM 03 0 9 8 7 6 5 4 3 2 1
CM PA 03 0 9 8 7 6 5 4 3 2 1

National Library of Canada Cataloguing in Publication Data

Mason, Adrienne
    Bats / written by Adrienne Mason ; illustrated by Nancy Gray Ogle.

(The Kids Can Press wildlife series)
Includes index.

ISBN 1-55337-524-6 (bound).
ISBN 1-55337-525-4 (pbk.)

1. Bats — Juvenile literature. I. Ogle, Nancy Gray
II. Title. III. Series: Kids Can Press wildlife series.

QL737.C5M38 2003   j599.4   C2002-905621-7

Kids Can Press is a *Corus*™ Entertainment company

Contents

Bats

Bats are animals that can fly, but they are not birds. They are small, furry animals that are active at night.

Bats are mammals. Mammals are warm-blooded animals that give birth to live babies. Baby mammals drink their mother's milk after they are born.

Bats are the only mammals that have wings and can fly. A few other mammals can glide but none can fly.

Some people believe bats are blind. This is an old story, but it is not true.

Big brown bat

Bats are very common. One-quarter of all mammal species are bats.

Kinds of bats

There are two main kinds of bats in the world: megabats and microbats. Mega means big and micro means small. Megabats are large bats that eat fruit or plants. Microbats are smaller and usually eat insects. They are the most common kind of bat.

Most microbats are about the size of a mouse, but the tiny bumblebee bat weighs less than a penny! Megabats are much larger. The giant flying fox has a wingspan of up to 2 m (6 feet). That is wider than you can stretch your arms.

Bumblebee bat

There are over 950 species of bats.

Flying fox

Where bats live

Bats live in forests, deserts, fields and even in cities. Bats can be found almost everywhere in the world, except Antarctica and very high mountaintops.

Megabats live in warm, tropical areas. There are no megabats in North America.

Epauletted bat

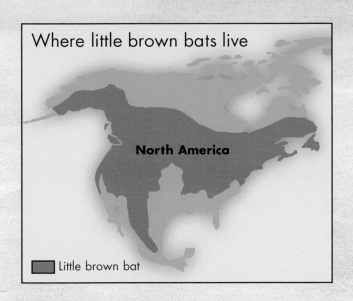

Where little brown bats live

North America

Little brown bat

A little brown bat eats up to 900 insects an hour.

Microbats live throughout the world. There are about 45 different species of microbats in North America. The little brown bat is one of the most common.

Little brown bat

Bat homes

Most bats rest during the day and hunt at night.
When they are not flying or feeding, bats need a
place to rest called a roost. Some bats rest alone,
but many live in large groups called colonies.
There can be thousands of bats in a colony.

Bats choose roosts that are well hidden and that
protect them from bad weather and other dangers.
A roost can be inside a hollow tree, a cave or in
the walls and roofs of buildings.

When bats rest, they hang upside down. This way
they can let go quickly and fly away if necessary.
Bats have special veins that keep the blood
moving through their bodies while they hang.

Straw-colored
fruit bats

Bats can use their wings as a raincoat or blanket by folding their wings around their bodies.

Some tiny bats even have roosts inside leaves or under tree bark.

11

Bats in winter

Some bats fly south in the fall when the weather cools. This is called migration. Bats fly to warmer areas because there is plenty of food. When bats migrate, they often travel along the same route year after year. In the spring, they fly north again.

Many bats in cool climates do not migrate in winter. They hibernate instead. Hibernating is like being in a deep sleep. During hibernation, bats cool their bodies. Their heart rate and breathing also slows down. This helps bats save energy and survive the winter.

Bats hibernate because there are fewer insects and plants for them to eat when it is cold. They do not eat or drink during their hibernation.

Bats hibernate in cool, dry places such as caves or old mines. They gather in large groups to keep each other warm.

Mexican free-tailed bats

Bat bodies

Bats, like this little brown bat, are light and built for flying.

Eyes

Megabats use their large eyes to see their food.

The eyes of microbats are very small, but they still use their eyes to get around and to find food.

Ears

Bats use large ears with many ridges and folds to hear a wide range of sounds.

Nose

A good sense of smell helps bats find food and their babies.

Teeth

Sharp teeth grasp insects or bite fruit.

Muscles

Strong muscles in the shoulders, chest and back help bats fly.

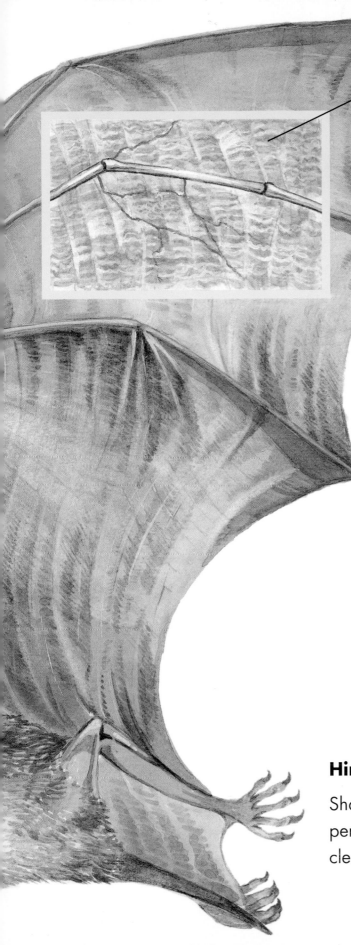

Wings

The wings are thin sheets of skin that are stretched between the bat's fingers. There is no fur on the wings.

Skeleton

Bat bones are very light to help bats fly. The fingers are long and slender. A hooked claw on the thumb is used to grip walls or other bats.

Hind feet

Sharp claws help bats grip their perches. Bats also use their claws to clean their fur and capture food.

How bats use sound and sight

Bats use sound to help them find food and avoid flying into things in the dark. They make very fast squeaks or "pings" of sound. Most of these sounds are very high-pitched and cannot be heard by people.

The sounds bounce off objects and echo back to the bat. From the echo, the bat can tell whether the object is food or something to avoid, like a tree or a wall. This use of sound to get around is called echolocation.

Even though their eyes are small, microbats do use their sense of sight. In places that are very familiar to them, microbats use sight more than sound.

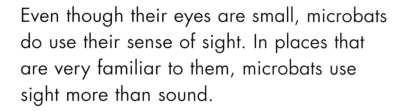

Townsend's big-eared bat

Megabats have large eyes and very good eyesight. Only one type of megabat uses echolocation.

Long-haired fruit bat

How bats move

Bats use their wings to fly. When a bat raises its wings, it moves up. When it pushes its wings down, the bat moves forward. Bats cannot glide or soar the way birds can.

Bats dive and turn very well in the air. They move like acrobats as they chase insects. Bats are even able to fly through a maze of tree branches.

Hoary bat

Bats sometimes crawl or hop on their wings.

Bat food

Many megabats feed on soft fruits such as bananas or mangoes. They crush the fruit in their mouths and drink the juice. They sometimes eat the mashed fruit, too.

Most microbats eat insects that fly at night. They use echolocation to find moths, mosquitoes, flies and beetles. Larger microbats can eat dragonflies, grasshoppers and even mice or lizards. Some bats use their wings like a baseball glove to catch insects.

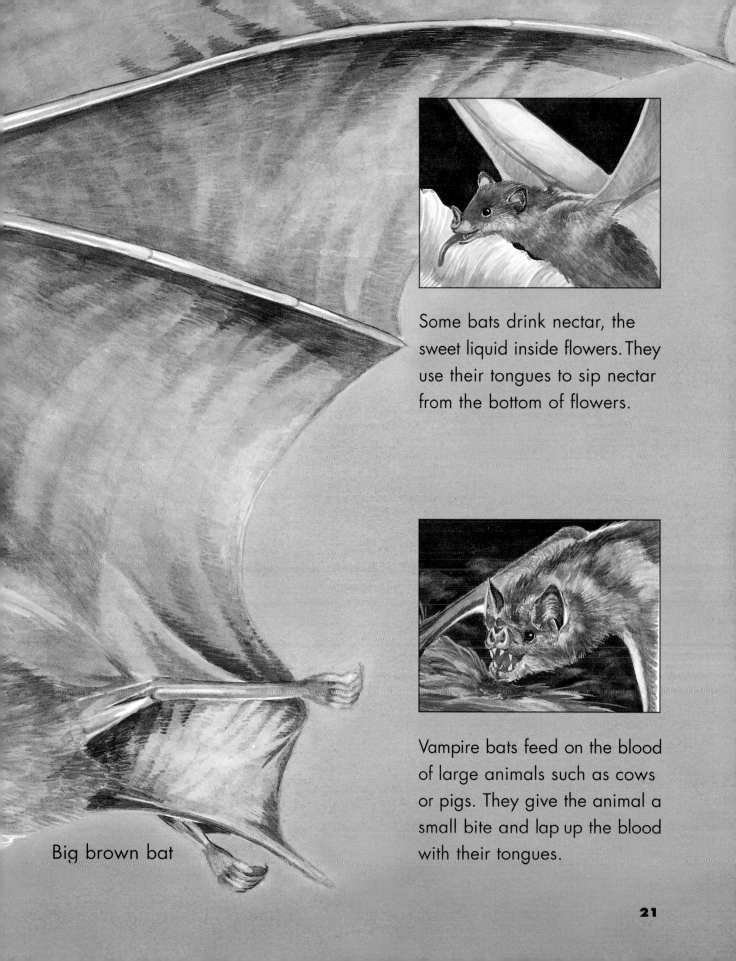

Some bats drink nectar, the sweet liquid inside flowers. They use their tongues to sip nectar from the bottom of flowers.

Vampire bats feed on the blood of large animals such as cows or pigs. They give the animal a small bite and lap up the blood with their tongues.

Big brown bat

How bats are born

A mother bat usually gives birth hanging upside down. The mother catches the baby in a flap of skin near her tail.

A baby bat is born blind and furless. After it is born, the baby crawls up to its mother's chest. The mother licks it clean, and within a few minutes the baby starts to drink milk from its mother's nipples.

Baby bats are born when it is warm and when there is a lot of food available. In North America, most bats are born in the spring.

Red bats

BAT FACT

Some female bats gather in nursery roosts to give birth.

How bats grow and learn

Newborn bats cannot fly so many mother bats carry their young babies with them. The baby clings to its mother's fur using the claws on its thumbs and feet.

Sometimes, mother bats will leave their babies clustered together in the roost when they go to feed. A mother bat finds her baby in the roost by listening for its high-pitched squeak or by smelling its scent.

Baby bats grow quickly. By the time they are one month old, baby bats have fur and their eyes are open. The babies are now as large as their mother. It is time for them to learn to fly.

Cave myotis bats

BAT FACT

Male bats do not take care of the babies.

At first, young bats hang from a perch and flap their wings to make them stronger. Next, the bats take small practice flights inside the roost. Before long, they are strong enough to fly and feed on their own.

How bats protect themselves

Bat enemies include birds of prey such as hawks, owls and falcons and other animals such as snakes, weasels, cats, raccoons, skunks and rats. Many animals try to catch bats as they leave their roost.

One way that bats protect themselves is by choosing a roost with a small opening. Hopefully, only bats can squeeze into the roost. Bats also keep safe by living in large groups. This way, a predator has more to choose from, so each bat is safer than if it was alone.

If a bat is attacked, it will usually try to fly away. Most bats are so small they would have difficulty winning a fight.

Even small birds, such as blue jays, can kill some types of bats.

Little brown bats

Since bats usually hang from the roof of their roosts, most enemies cannot reach them. Few animals can climb high enough to catch the bats.

Bats and people

Some people are afraid of bats, but bats help us in many ways.

Bats help control the number of insects in nature. They eat many insects that we consider pests, such as mosquitoes.

Nectar-eating bats carry pollen from plant to plant. Spreading pollen helps plants with fruit and flowers to grow.

Fruit-eating bats help spread plant seeds. They drop seeds in their body waste as they fly. These seeds grow into new plants.

Bat homes are sometimes destroyed when people cut down trees or destroy old buildings. But many people are trying to help save bats. They tell others about all the good things that bats can do. They also work to protect bat homes and habitat.

Some people put
special bat boxes in
their yards to give
bats a place to roost.

Bats around the world

Microbats live on every continent except Antarctica.
Megabats live in Africa, Asia and Australia.

Microbats

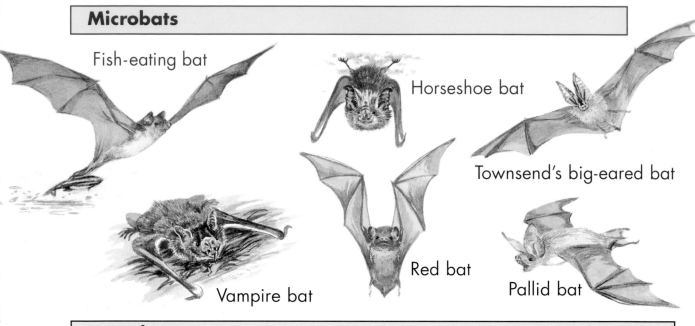

Fish-eating bat

Horseshoe bat

Townsend's big-eared bat

Vampire bat

Red bat

Pallid bat

Megabats

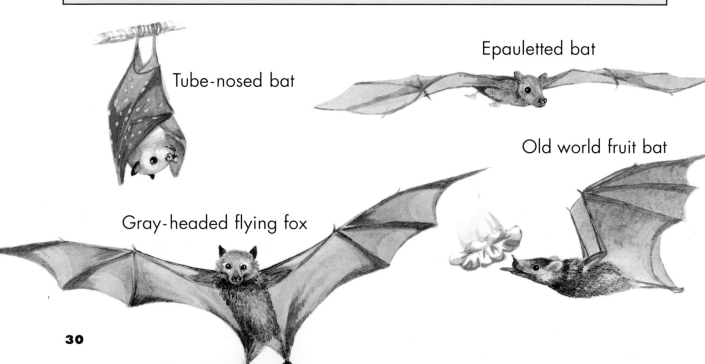

Tube-nosed bat

Epauletted bat

Old world fruit bat

Gray-headed flying fox

Words to know

colonies: large groups of bats that live together

echolocation: the ability to use sound to locate food and other objects

hibernation: a deep sleep during the winter. Hibernation helps animals save energy and survive the winter in cold climates.

mammal: a warm-blooded animal with fur, whose babies are born live and fed mother's milk

megabats: large bats that usually eat fruit or other plants

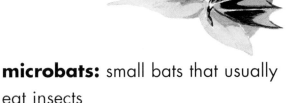

microbats: small bats that usually eat insects

migration: to travel from place to place as the seasons change

nectar: a sweet liquid found inside flowers

roost: the place where bats rest

Index